Animal Antics

Compiled by Wendy Body and Pat Edwards

Acknowledgements

We are grateful to the following for permission to reproduce copyright material: Andersen Press Limited for the story 'Crazy Charlie' from *Crazy Charlie* by Ruth Brown (pub. Andersen Press 1979); A & C Black (Publishers) Limited for the story 'A Souvenir From The Zoo' from *Trouble With Animals* by Jeremy Strong (1980); The Blackie Publishing Group for the story 'Marmalade Atkins and the Night Conversation' from *Marmalade and Rufus* by Andrew Davies (1979); the author, Patricia Lauber for her story 'Animal Trainer' from *Clarence Turns Seadog* Copyright © 1959 Patricia Lauber.

Illustrators include: Dave Parkins pp. 4–15; Judy Leech pp. 16–19; Melissa Webb pp. 20–35; Lorraine Ellis pp. 36–7; Bucket pp. 38–47; Ruth Brown pp. 48–61; Mike Gordon p. 62; Denise Carter pp. 63–4.

Contents

Marmalade Atkins and the Night Conversation

Marmalade Atkins is not a nice girl and Rufus is a pretty diabolical donkey. So if you only like stories about sweet little girls and gentle, lovable donkeys, this probably isn't for you!

Suddenly Marmalade was awake. She sat straight up in bed and listened. Someone was moving about downstairs. It wasn't her mother, whose high heels echoed on the oak floors like whipcracks. It wasn't her father, who slouched. It was someone who wore very heavy boots, with metal caps or something like that on, and this someone was moving with a tread so heavy that the walls vibrated. It must be a very big burglar.

Now most girls would be terrified if they heard this sort of thing. They would huddle down under the bedclothes and tell themselves they were dreaming, they would shiver and shake, they would hug their teddies. But Marmalade, as we have seen, was not like most girls. She had often wished she could meet a burglar and ask him about his life, which must be an exciting and interesting one, she thought. In fact she had sometimes thought that she would like to be a burglar when she grew up.

4

Very quietly Marmalade Atkins slipped out of bed and put her slippers on. It was important not to disturb the burglar, or he might run off without taking anything. There were several things that Marmalade wanted burgled. Her Brownie uniform was one of them. And there were several china models of dancers belonging to her mother on the mantelpiece; their soppy expressions had got on Marmalade's wick for years, but perhaps a burglar would think them worth taking. And if he had a van, she thought eagerly, he might agree to take the Encyclopaedia Britannica, Every Child's Passport to Success. Horrible great lurking thing. Marmalade tiptoed to the door and listened.

The burglar seemed to have stopped moving around. And very faintly Marmalade could hear the sound of the television. She was impressed. This must be a very cool burglar, taking a rest to watch telly before getting on with his work. If he was nicely settled, now would be the time to go down and introduce herself.

She tiptoed down the stairs and across the hall. The living room door was open a tiny crack. Marmalade Atkins put her eye to the crack. Yes, the telly was on. Green, black, red, flashes of brown. Horses. It must be the Horse of the Year Show. And sitting watching it, slumped in the middle of the sofa, was the burglar.

Most of the burglar was hidden by the high back of the sofa, but the bits that Marmalade could see looked very strange indeed. The burglar seemed to be wearing a flat check cap very like one that Marmalade's father had, and underneath the cap some sort of reddish woolly thing like a Balaclava helmet. But it wasn't an ordinary Balaclava helmet. It had ears. Long ears. Long ears that stuck up straight in the air. Like a donkey's ears.

Marmalade paused and held her breath, and over the sound of the television she heard a wheezy creaking sound, halfway between a chuckle and someone sitting on a set of bagpipes. Then a hoarse voice, like a voice that hadn't been used for years, said:

"Daft'oss."

Marmalade opened the door wide and stepped in.

The burglar turned.

"Evenin', Marmalade Atkins," said the burglar.

It was Rufus.

Rufus did not seem in the least shy about being caught
lolling on the sofa. He seemed perfectly at home. He
nodded amiably at Marmalade and gestured with his
hoof at the bag of apples by his side. Marmalade took
one without thinking, and started eating it.

"That's my girl," said Rufus, and turned back to the
television. Marmalade decided to assert herself.

"Now look here, Rufus," she said. "I'm not your girl,
you're my donkey! Who d'you think you are, coming in
here and rolling your great hairy body about on our sofa,
and eating our apples and watching our television, and
wearing my father's hat — you look *daft* in it — and
talking, donkeys don't *talk*, don't you *know* that, and
generally carrying on as if you own the place. It simply
won't do. What's your game?"

Rufus spat an apple pip into the fire.

"Do own the place. Cheeky monkey."

Marmalade was enraged. She didn't seem to be
impressing him at all. He had even turned back to watch
the telly.

"Rufus!" she shouted.

Rufus did his wheezy chuckle again.

"Look at them daft horses," he said. "They haven't got
the sense they was born with."

Marmalade began to feel that she was on the losing side in this conversation, which was an unusual feeling for her.

"What d'you mean, you own the place?" she said crossly. "My father paid a lot of money for it."

"Don't mean a thing to me, Marmalade," said Rufus. "I was here before he was."

"Right! Right!" shouted Marmalade. "You came with the farm, you did, he bought you with it, he bought you for me, so you're my donkey, see? Get it? *Eh?*"

Rufus turned his head slowly and looked at Marmalade as she stood there in her nightie all red in the face and stamping her foot. Marmalade began to feel rather silly, and stopped stamping.

"I'm me own donkey," he said. "Always was, always will be."

Marmalade couldn't find an answer to that one, though she racked her brains till they hurt. She thought she might think better if she sat down, so she sat on a little stool by Rufus's feet, and looked up at him. He looked very big and old and clever, and she felt weak and small.

"What about all this talking then?" she said grumpily. "How long have you been able to talk?"

"Always," said Rufus. "Nothing to it."

"Ho," said Marmalade Atkins craftily. "Why haven't you done any talking before then?"

"Never saw the need of it," said Rufus. "People round here are such a lot of fools, I wouldn't waste me breath on them."

Marmalade thought about this for a minute or two. And then she said in a small and thoughtful voice:

"But you've started to talk to me. Why did you want to talk to me?"

For the first time Rufus paused before answering. He shifted his huge gingery bulk this way and that on the sofa, leaving several coarse ginger hairs and a damp muddy stain on the flowered chintz. It was almost as if he was embarrassed.

"Like your style," he said grudgingly. "Like the way you handle yourself."

Marmalade had stopped feeling angry. Instead she was feeling very strange. Rufus liked her style, whatever that meant. He didn't want to talk to her mother, however smart and good at bridge she was, and he didn't want to talk to her father, however rich and absent-minded he was, and he clearly didn't want to talk to big softy Cherith Ponsonby, however goody-goody she was. He wanted to talk to Marmalade Atkins, because he liked her style. Nobody had ever liked Marmalade's style before, whatever that meant, and it felt very good to know that Rufus did.

But there must be a catch in it somewhere. Life, Marmalade knew, was like that. She thought for a minute or two and then decided she knew what it was.

"Listen, Rufus," she said. "You're not one of those talking animals who come up to bad children in fairy stories and make them feel all soft and soppy inside so that they turn into big softies and goody-goodies like Cherith Ponsonby? You're not one of those animals, are you, because if you are, *bad luck*!"

"No, Marmalade Atkins," said Rufus, "I'm not one of them sort of animals at all."

Marmalade did some more thinking.

"What sort of animal are you then?" she said.

"I'm an animal to be reckoned with," said Rufus proudly.

"I knew that," said Marmalade.

"Right then," said Rufus. He turned back to the television as if the conversation was over. Marmalade waited a long time but nothing else happened. She was getting used to sitting in the living room late at night with a talking donkey in a checked cap. She hoped that this was not all there was going to be to it. She tried to be patient and wait for the next thing, but the next thing seemed a long time coming and she was not used to being patient. In the end she had to say something.

"What's it like?" she said.

"What's what like?" said Rufus irritably. The Horses of the Year were having a jump-off and he seemed to be getting involved despite himself.

"Being a donkey," said Marmalade.

"Terrible," said Rufus briefly.

"Why?" said Marmalade.

Rufus turned wearily away from the telly and fixed his sleepy eyes on her.

"Well," he said, "How would you like folks to call you a sweet little thing, and put silly hats on you, and try to get on your back and ride round on you, and put you in a cold old stable with a couple of daft young ponies without *ever* once asking if you wouldn't rather have a bed like what they've got? Eh?"

"I wouldn't like it at all," said Marmalade. "I wouldn't put up with it."

"Neither do I," said Rufus. "I takes liberties. But plenty of donkeys don't."

On the television, a rider called Buster Creighton incurred four faults and was eliminated from the final round. Rufus gave a brief guffaw and turned back to Marmalade.

"Added to which," he said, "I'm an old donkey, I am. Know how long I been on this farm?"

"No," said Marmalade, walking into it.

"Donkey's years!" roared Rufus, falling about laughing.

There was a sound of splintering wood from inside the sofa and one of the arms fell sideways and sagged pathetically towards the floor.

"Oh dear, oh dear," said Rufus, not looking sorry at all. "Never mind. Not often I get a good laff."

Marmalade wondered who would get blamed for the broken sofa. She did not need to wonder long. It would be her, of course, unless she could spin a story about a bunch of Arabs coming looking for her father and overloading the sofa with their camels or something. Yes, no problem: she would think of a good story. Anything would seem more likely than the truth.

"No, to be serious," said Rufus, "the thing about being a donkey is you live so long. After the first ninety years or so, folk start getting on your wick. You feel like taking a few liberties and putting yourself about a bit."

"I've seen you at it," said Marmalade.

"What d'you think of it?" said Rufus.

"I like it," said Marmalade. "I like to take a few liberties myself."

"I've been watching you," said Rufus. "I reckon you and I could have a bit of fun together."

"What sort of fun?" said Marmalade Atkins.

"All sorts of fun," said Rufus. "Take that Buster Creighton, for one. He's had it coming to him for a bit. He wants pushing over and standing on, he does."

Marmalade stared at her donkey in admiration and awe.

"You mean you're going to knock Buster Creighton down and stand on him?"

"Course I am," said Rufus, "I'm going to give that Buster Creighton a right seeing to, no problem. No hurry. I can bide my time. Course, they'll hush it up, like when I pushed that Mark Philpotts in the manure heap. He's another right one for getting on horses' backs and making them jump over things. I can't abide that. Makes me want to knock 'em down and stand on 'em."

"And when you want to, you do," said Marmalade.

"Well, that's obvious," said Rufus. Marmalade felt a deep surge of affection for Rufus. She had never met anyone who felt like she did before.

"Do you do anything else, or do you just knock people down and stand on them?" she said. "Not that I'm criticising, of course."

"That's not the half of what I gets up to," said Rufus mysteriously.

"What else do you get up to?" said Marmalade.

"Well," said Rufus. "I gets dressed up and I goes out . . ."

"And?" said Marmalade.

"And I puts myself about a bit," said Rufus modestly.

"But *how*?" said Marmalade. She simply had to know.

"All sorts of ways," said Rufus vaguely. Marmalade felt let down, and Rufus seemed to sense it.

"Come and see for yourself if you like, one of these nights."

"Can I really?"

"Often felt like a bit of company," said Rufus.

"But how will I wake up?" said Marmalade.

"Oh, you'll wake up. I'll be down here. You sneak down the stairs like, and I'll be waiting for you, and then we'll go out, and by heck we'll put ourselves about a bit."

That was the last thing Marmalade Atkins remembered of the strange night conversation. The next thing she knew, she was lying awake in bed, it was morning, birds were singing outside the windows, and somewhere in the distance was the familiar sound of Rufus hee-hawing his morning greeting to the world.

How disappointing. How infuriatingly *feeble*. She must have dreamed the whole lot. The Horse of the Year Show, the checked cap, the talking donkey, everything. Why did dreams have to be so much more interesting than real life? And what a fool she had been to think it was all really true. No, Rufus was just an ordinary donkey. Diabolical, but just a donkey. Oh, well, back to normal. Grr.

In a thoroughly bad mood, Marmalade got out of bed, put her slippers on, and stamped down the stairs to breakfast. Her mother was sitting at the table looking at her very coldly. Now what? thought Marmalade grimly.

"Marmalade Atkins," said her mother. "I have a bone to pick with you."

"Oh," said Marmalade.

"Yes," said her mother.

"I want you to explain that disgusting mess in the lounge."

Marmalade felt her heart give a thump.

"What mess?" she said, hoping against hope.

"You know very well what mess!" shouted her mother, suddenly losing her temper, and she grabbed Marmalade's arm, yanked her to her feet, and propelled her into the lounge.

"There! That mess!" she screamed, pointing at the sofa.

Written by Andrew Davies,
illustrated by Dave Parkins

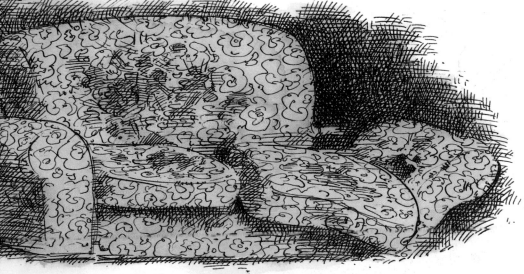

You can read more about Marmalade in
Marmalade and Rufus by Andrew Davies,
published by Blackie

Diary of a New Pet

SATURDAY

10:00 am Left pet shop with new owners. There are four of them, two big ones and two little ones. The little boy one tasted best. We got into something called a car. The two little owners fought over who was to hold me. The girl won.

10:15 am Was sick. After that, no one wanted to hold me.

10:30 am Arrived at new home. Had race around rooms with girl and boy and made puddle in middle of carpet. The big owner called Mum seemed upset.

12:30 pm Everyone but me had meal. I was upset.

1:00 pm Big row about what to call me. Everyone got upset.

1:30 pm All the owners went out. I was left alone in house. Main room now has wall-to-wall newspaper. Was careful not to make a puddle on the newspaper.

1:40 pm Cried broken-heartedly, but no one came.

1:45 pm Found two books on low table. Interesting taste, but I couldn't eat much.

1:50 pm Now very thirsty. Found a water jar with flowers stuck in it. Accidentally tipped it over. Ate flowers, but didn't like them much.

17

2:00 pm Felt sleepy. Pulled pale pink velvet cushion down from chair and made myself comfortable. Now feeling very lonely so chewed corner to cheer myself up.

4:30 pm Everyone came back. Owner called Mum was very upset. I wonder why?

5:00 pm Had first meal. Not very hungry but got it all down.

5:05 pm Ate cat's dinner. Don't like fish.

5:30 pm Taken outside by girl and boy owners. Had great game rushing round on the lawn. Got excited and yapped a lot. Old lady put head over fence, looked at me and said "Oh, no!". Ate some more flowers.

5:35 pm Went inside and was sick. Mum's turn to say "Oh, no!". (I think that's my name.) She was upset again.

18

6:30 pm	Everyone but me had meal. I was upset again.
7:30 pm	We all watched TV. I find I can only sleep comfortably on Mum's lap.
9:00 pm	Put out to sleep in basket in cold room.
10:00 pm	One hour of crying seems to have upset everyone.
10:10 pm	Settled down on end of Mum's bed. Have decided I love her best and will always sleep here. Owner called Dad now seems upset and said "Oh, no!" I wonder why?

Pat Edwards
Illustrated by Judy Leech

19

Animal Trainer

Brian and Sis and their dog Clarence are staying with Aunt Jo for the holidays. They have made friends with Mr. Webster, who has a talking parrot called Polly. One day they are visiting their new friends . . .

"I wish we had a talking parrot," Brian said. He paused. "Or what would be better yet, I wish Clarence could talk." He turned to Mr. Webster. "Can dogs learn to talk?"

"I don't really know," Mr. Webster said. "But surely you don't want a talking dog. If I were you, I'd leave well enough alone."

"Besides," I pointed out, "Clarence can almost talk. We always know what he's thinking and what he wants. Look at him now."

Clarence had discovered a box of cookies on the ground near the table. He looked at the box. Then he looked at Mr. Webster and back again at the cookie box. He licked his whiskers and sniffed in the direction of the cookies. He looked again at Mr. Webster.

"Obviously he wants a cookie," Mr. Webster said. Clarence's tail wagged at the word. Mr. Webster passed the cookies to us and then gave one to Clarence. "You're a good dog, Clarence," he said. "You deserve a reward for chasing that cat."

"Could Clarence's reward be learning to talk?" Brian asked. "Please?"

"I don't know —" Mr. Webster began.

"I mean, could you try to teach him?" Brian went on. "You taught Polly, and Clarence is very intelligent. Would you try?"

Mr. Webster chewed his lower lip and studied Clarence. "I supp—"

At that moment it happened.

Clarence looked from the cookie box to Mr. Webster and said quite plainly, "Cookies." Brian and I gasped. Mr. Webster shook his head, "Cookies, *please*"

He and Clarence gazed into each other's eyes. Clarence licked his lips, hesitated, and finally got it out: "Cookies, please."

"That's a good dog," Mr. Webster said. Brian and I were speechless.

COOKIES PLEASE

Mr. Webster opened the box and fed Clarence two cookies. Then he put the box in the house, saying, "That's enough for one day."

"I don't," Brian said, "I don't —" He was so astonished that he couldn't get the words out.

Mr. Webster understood. "An animal, like a child, may be ready to talk, but doesn't until something special happens and starts him. Probably it was meeting Polly that started Clarence. He listened to her and thought if she could talk so could he."

"Will Clarence go on talking?" I asked.

"I should think so, though he'll need expert help."

"Could you — would you help him?" Brian asked. "It would be wonderful if Clarence could talk. Please help him."

"Well," Mr. Webster said, "I'm a very busy man — I'm writing a book. But I guess I could spare the time to help Clarence, if that's what you really want."

"More than anything," Brian said.

"Clever girl, Polly!" Polly squawked. Then she said, "Foaming action, foaming action, foaming action! Ha-ha-ha!"

23

"That reminds me," Mr. Webster said, walking us toward his gate. "Talking animals should be kept away from radios and TV sets so they don't start learning the commercials."

We thought it was probably too late in Clarence's case. But Brian was bubbling over with ideas about putting Clarence *on* television and earning thousands and thousands of pounds and all the things we were going to buy with the money. But he agreed when I suggested that we keep Clarence's talking a secret until Clarence was ready to perform in public. Otherwise, of course, people would just laugh when we said we had a talking dog. And Clarence hates being laughed at.

For the first few days everything went well. We took Clarence to Mr. Webster's each morning for a lesson. And once he'd started talking, Clarence made rapid progress. For example, Mr. Webster and Clarence would sit looking at each other, and the conversation would go something like this:

MR. WEBSTER: Well, Clarence, how are you today?

CLARENCE: Hungry.

MR. WEBSTER: Hungry? Why, you're always hungry. Don't they feed you at home?

CLARENCE: They forget.

MR. WEBSTER: You poor little dog! You're probably starving.

BRIAN: Clarence, that's not so. We never forget to feed you.

CLARENCE   (*looking reproachfully at Brian*): Poor starving little dog.

BRIAN   (*indignantly*):   You're not! You're the one who has forgotten.

CLARENCE: Can't forget hunger.

MR. WEBSTER: Well, we can't have that. Would you like a cookie?

CLARENCE   (*jumping to his feet*):   Would I!

And there the lesson would end. Mr. Webster would pass the cookies. Then Clarence would wander off to visit Polly while we chatted.

Brian was a little disturbed about some of the things Clarence said. On the third day, as soon as Clarence was out of earshot, Brian complained, "We don't forget to feed him! Why does he keep saying that?"

"Well," Mr. Webster said, "it's probably hard for him to remember when he had his last meal."

Brian was still brooding. "What will people think if he goes around saying that?"

Mr. Webster shrugged. "That's the trouble with talking animals. There's no telling what they'll say."

A slight cloud passed over Brian's face. I knew what he was thinking. Suppose Clarence told millions of people in the TV audience that he was a poor starving little dog. I could just imagine the kind of letters we'd receive from people accusing us of taking the poor little dog's earnings and then not giving him enough to eat.

26

Meanwhile, Mr. Webster had a problem of his own. Clarence and Polly were becoming very good friends and they'd worked up a game that they played. Polly called, "Here, pussy, pussy, pussy! Nice pussy!" And when the cat came, Clarence chased it and barked while Polly laughed. Mr. Webster wasn't very happy about the game. "Polly's going to be sorry," he said.

As a matter of fact, we weren't completely happy
either. You might think it would be wonderful to have
a talking dog, but somehow it changes things.

First, temptation became too strong for Brian. We
had promised Mr. Webster that we wouldn't try to
make Clarence talk at home. Mr. Webster said it
would confuse him to have more than one teacher.
Also, he didn't want Clarence to overdo talking and
strain his throat.

This seemed very sensible. So I was angry when I
came upon Brian behind the garage, trying to make
Clarence talk. Brian was sitting on the ground,
staring into Clarence's eyes the way Mr. Webster did.
"What's your name?" he was saying over and over
again to Clarence. When Clarence didn't answer,
Brian said helpfully, "Is it Albert? Is it George? Is it
Clarence?" At the last question, Clarence wagged his
tail.

Tiptoeing away, I decided to teach Brian a lesson. When I saw him a little later, I said, "What do you mean trying to make Clarence talk when you promised not to?"

Brian flushed. "How did you find out?"

I looked Brian straight in the eye. "Clarence told me."

Brian's jaw dropped. Then he recovered and said, "You broke the promise, too."

"No, I didn't. I didn't ask him to speak. He just came and told me."

Brian glared at poor Clarence. "Tattletale!" he said and stamped off.

At first I was very pleased. I started to share the joke with Clarence, but then I thought better of it. I didn't want him blurting out the truth in front of Brian and Mr. Webster. My pleasure changed to unhappiness. Brian and I have always shared secrets with Clarence and talked to him when we needed to get something off our chests. But if Clarence was going to talk, we'd have to stop.

Clarence sensed my feelings and thought he had done something wrong. He crept off and spent the rest of the afternoon with Aunt Jo.

Aunt Jo also knew there was something wrong. She came to find us before dinner and said, "Now, children, make up. You won't enjoy your meal in a bad temper."

"We're not really in a bad temper," I said. "We just —"

"Yes, you are," Aunt Jo said, smiling. "I know. A little bird told me."

Brian and I both looked at Clarence.

Clarence shrank back against Aunt Jo, puzzled and hurt.

Just then Uncle Matt arrived. "Heard there was roast beef for dinner," he boomed. "So I thought I'd stop by and see if any invitations were being handed out."

"Gracious," Aunt Jo said, "how did you find that out?"

"Word gets around, eh, Clarence?" Uncle Matt winked at him.

That was too much for Brian. "It's not fair!" he burst out. "Clarence talks to everybody except me. I hate this. I wish we'd never started it."

"Here, here," Uncle Matt said. "What's all this?"

30

We told him, and somehow just the telling made me feel better. At the end, Brian said, "You see, it *isn't* fair. Why should Clarence talk to Sis and you and Aunt Jo but not to me?"

I confessed. "Clarence didn't talk to me. I made it up to teach you a lesson."

Aunt Jo said, "And he didn't talk to me. Goodness, nobody had to tell me there was something wrong. It was written all over your faces."

We all looked at Uncle Matt. He grinned and said, "I could smell the roast beef practically up at my place. An old bachelor is likely to be pretty good at sniffing out a tasty dinner."

Brian put his arms around Clarence. "I'm sorry for all the mean things I was thinking," he said.

Clarence was very happy to be out of disgrace. He nibbled Brian's ears and bit him gently on the nose.

"I wish," I said, "that there was some way we could teach Clarence not to talk any more."

"So do I," Brian said. "He was just right when he was almost talking but not quite saying anything."

Uncle Matt nodded. "I agree. Tell you what. Why don't you go along and see Charlie Webster after dinner? Tell him how you feel and ask him to help you."

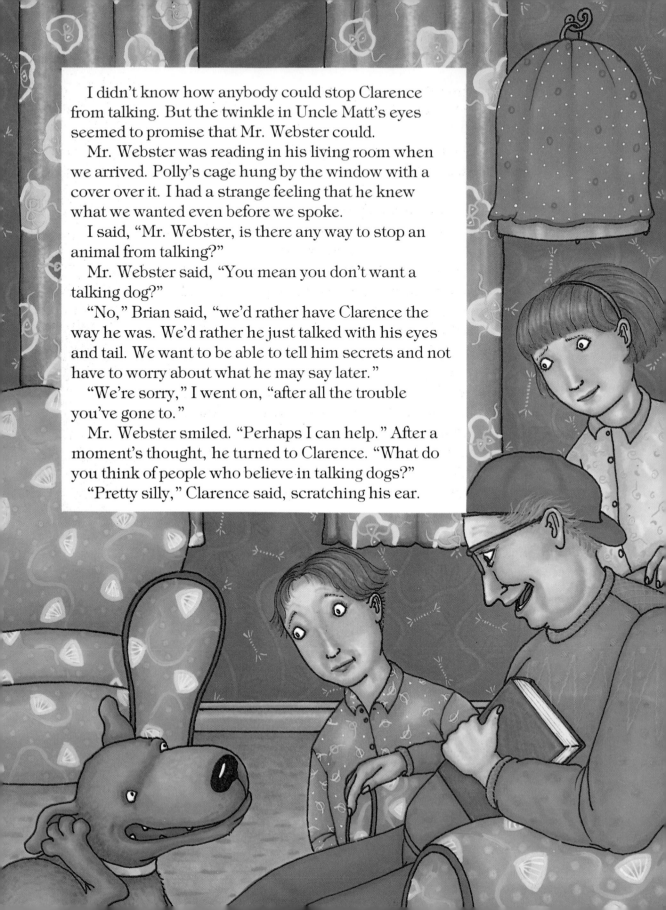

I didn't know how anybody could stop Clarence from talking. But the twinkle in Uncle Matt's eyes seemed to promise that Mr. Webster could.

Mr. Webster was reading in his living room when we arrived. Polly's cage hung by the window with a cover over it. I had a strange feeling that he knew what we wanted even before we spoke.

I said, "Mr. Webster, is there any way to stop an animal from talking?"

Mr. Webster said, "You mean you don't want a talking dog?"

"No," Brian said, "we'd rather have Clarence the way he was. We'd rather he just talked with his eyes and tail. We want to be able to tell him secrets and not have to worry about what he may say later."

"We're sorry," I went on, "after all the trouble you've gone to."

Mr. Webster smiled. "Perhaps I can help." After a moment's thought, he turned to Clarence. "What do you think of people who believe in talking dogs?"

"Pretty silly," Clarence said, scratching his ear.

Brian stared at Clarence. "But —"

"And what's the best way to stop a dog from talking?"

Clarence picked out a comfortable chair and jumped into it. "Stop believing." He yawned and lay down.

"Oh!" I said, suddenly understanding.

"*You're* doing it," Brian said. "Clarence isn't talking at all. You're a ventro — a ventri —"

"A ventriloquist," Mr. Webster finished. And then, so we wouldn't be ashamed of having been fooled, he went on and told us stories about other people he'd fooled, making his voice come from all parts of the room. We had such fun that we didn't mind at all.

The next day, to show we were really still friends, we went back to see Mr. Webster. He was having lunch outdoors and Polly was squawking "Foaming action, foaming action," over and over again.

When Polly saw Clarence, she stopped the commercial and said, "Good dog, Clarence. Good dog, Clarence," which she'd picked up from Mr. Webster.

Clarence wagged his tail, but he was much more interested in Mr. Webster's lunch than in Polly. He took a seat beside Mr. Webster and looked hopefully at him.

"Would you like a cookie?" Mr. Webster asked Clarence.

Clarence pricked up his ears and wagged his tail, as good as saying, "Would I!"

Mr. Webster reached for the box.

Polly was still trying to catch Clarence's attention. "Nice pussy! Here, pussy, pussy, pussy!"

"Polly, stop that!" Mr. Webster snapped, opening the box.

"Here, pussy, pus — awk!" The cat had jumped to the table.

A burst of barking followed, and the cat fled.

"Ha-ha-ha!" Polly laughed.

"It won't be so funny when Clarence has gone back to Connecticut," Mr. Webster told Polly.

"But Clarence didn't bark," Brian said.

Mr. Webster looked down. Clarence was still sitting at his feet and staring at the cookie box.

We all looked at Polly.

Polly preened her feathers. "Nice pussy," she said — and barked.

There were no two ways about it. Clarence had taught Polly to bark. Instead of our having a talking dog, Mr. Webster had a barking bird.

Patricia Lauber
Illustrated by Melissa Webb

CHOOSING AN OWNER

Rules for pets

1 Be firm right from the start. Insist on 5 meals a day with snacks in-between.

2 If a dog, remember most owners need exercise. But you don't need to go with them unless you feel like it.

3 Dogs must protect their owners from all strangers. Postmen are trying to steal the letter box, everyone else is probably trying to steal the front door.

4 Choose the chair you like best for daytime sleeping. If an owner takes it away from you, sigh a lot and look sad. As soon as the phone or doorbell rings, grab it back.

5 If a cruel, selfish owner insists on putting you out in the cold at night, howl mournfully until the neighbours complain.

6 When owners get cross, try these tips:

   a Birds: sing beautifully or cock your head on one side and say "Pretty boy!" They like to be told this.

   b Cats: rub against their legs when it's not meal time or jump into a lap and start purring.

   c Dogs: lots of sloppy, wet licks should do the trick.

   d Rabbits, white rats and mice: stroke your whiskers and try to look cute and helpless.

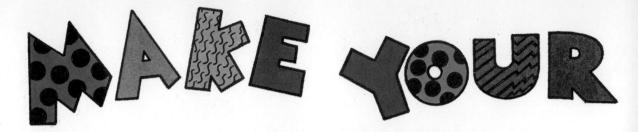

What you need: Pieces of light cardboard that will bend easily.
Paint and brushes.
Felt-tip pens for adding details.

Method:

Step 1 Take a piece of cardboard and bend in half.

Step 2

Draw your animal on one half so that part of the design runs along the fold.

Step 3 Hold the folded cardboard, and cut out your animal. Be careful not to cut the fold.

Step 4 Colour your new pet any way you like and add nose, whiskers, eyes, mouth, etc.

You can make a whole menagerie if you like.

Fold

Extras you can add:
cotton wool tail to rabbit
whiskers made from cotton thread
paper feathers to bird
toy eyes

Fold

Fold

Fold

A Souvenir from the Zoo

Tom desperately wants a pet — this is only one of his many adventures when he sets out to find an animal of his own.

Dad took a day off work. Mum thought that if they all went to the zoo, perhaps Tom would see enough to satisfy his need for a pet. Certainly Tom and Jane were excited by the idea.

"We haven't been to the zoo for ages," Jane said. "Do you remember the last time we went Dad? The monkeys thought Tom was one of them and they tried to pull him into their cage!" Tom went bright red.

"They didn't!" he said hotly, and he hurried upstairs to get his duffle-bag. It was true, though. On their last visit Tom had stood against the monkey cage so that Dad could take a photograph. One of the monkeys had slipped a long hairy arm through the bars and grabbed a handful of Tom's hair. He had felt very foolish. Jane, of course, thought it was the best photo in the album.

It was a warm day and Mum and Dad had made a picnic lunch. They all piled into the car. Nicola and her brother Paul called out from over the road to ask where they were going. Jane leant out of the car window and shouted back.

"We won't be long. We're just taking Tom back to the zoo. The monkeys have asked if they can have him back."

"Jane! Don't shout like that," said Dad. "Pull your head in before it gets knocked off."

"I'll knock it off," murmured Tom. Mum turned round.

"Now look, you two, we're going to enjoy ourselves, so we'll have none of that."

Jane looked at Tom and Tom looked at Jane. They both raised their eyebrows as if they were terribly surprised Mum should think they would ever quarrel with each other. They settled down and watched the traffic until they reached the zoo. Once the car was parked, they rushed off, trying to see everything at once.

Jane took great delight in showing Tom a fat
boa-constrictor snoozing in the reptile house. The
snake was curled round a lump of dead wood.

"It's probably just eaten," said Jane. "I expect it
swallowed the keeper."

"I bet they haven't got a blue whale here," Tom said. Jane giggled and approached the keeper on duty.

"Excuse me, but is there a blue whale here at all?" Jane tried to look angelic. The keeper smiled and shook his head.

"No, Miss. I'm sorry. We haven't got a blue whale. Bit too big, you see."

Jane seemed disappointed. "Oh dear. I wanted to show my brother. Well, have you got a green whale?"

"Green whale!" The keeper frowned. He didn't know whether or not Jane was pulling his leg.

"Or a pink one?" suggested Jane, but she could not keep a straight face any longer and she began to laugh. Tom wished Jane would not do such awful things but he could not help laughing all the same. The keeper sighed heavily and walked off, trying to look important.

Mum and Dad caught up with them and they decided to eat. Mum and Dad were both rather tired and they sat on the grass among the cages after lunch and told the children they could look round by themselves.

"But don't go too far away," warned Mum.

At first they went around together, returning
every now and then to tell Mum and Dad excitedly of
their latest finds. But Mum and Dad soon fell asleep
and Tom and Jane quarrelled. Tom went off in a huff
to explore for himself.

He passed by the penguin pool and stopped for a
moment to watch them being fed. His eye was
caught by a rather small, seedy-looking bird that
stood by itself in one corner. The keeper threw some
fish into the pool and soon the fish had all gone.
Only Tom noticed that the small lonely penguin had
not eaten a scrap. His heart was filled with pity for
it. It must have been abandoned by the other
penguins. Tom went round to where the poor
penguin stood moping beside a low wall.

He leant over and talked softly to the bird. "You
poor thing. Haven't you got any friends? Neither
have I. Don't you like fish? Neither do I — unless

they're fish fingers. I don't suppose they give you fish fingers here, do they?" The little bird did not seem to be very interested in Tom's chatter. It just stood there looking very sorry for itself. Tom wished he could do something to help it.

The keepers left the penguins and went to bath the elephants. The crowd followed. This gave Tom his chance. He was surprised how easy it was to catch a penguin. After all the difficulty he'd had in the past, he was sure this one would kick up a fuss too. He leant over the wall, put both arms carefully round the bird, which didn't even struggle, and slipped it into his duffle-bag. Then he walked quickly away.

43

Jane was already back with Mum and Dad and they were wondering what had happened to Tom when he arrived, carefully carrying his bag. It was time to go, Mum said. She handed a pile of uneaten picnic food to Tom and told him to put it in his bag.

"Come on, Tom, hurry up," said Dad. Tom seemed to be taking an awfully long time. He was putting the food in with great care, keeping one hand over the top of the bag, just in case the penguin decided to fly out. Tom could not remember if penguins could fly or not.

"Buck up, Tom!" moaned Mum.

"He's probably got something in there," joked Jane. "He's probably got a baby camel or a boa-constrictor in there. You know he wants a pet."

Tom glared at her and told her to be quiet. He slung the bag over his shoulder just to prove she was wrong. There was a small squeak from deep inside. Luckily nobody heard.

The journey home seemed to last an age. Tom sat quite still, nursing the duffle-bag on his lap, hoping the penguin would not choose this time to start wriggling or squawking.

"Can I have another sandwich?" asked Jane, halfway home.

"They're in Tom's bag," Mum said.

Jane leant over and started to fiddle with the top of the bag. Tom snatched it back, shouting angrily. "Leave it alone!"

"She only wants a sandwich," said Dad.

"I'll get it out, then."

"But you don't know what kind I want," Jane complained.

"I'll get it out," insisted Tom. Mum sighed.

"Tell him what kind you want and let him get it for you."

"I want a cucumber one with no salt or pepper on it," Jane said.

Tom slid his hand into the bag, keeping the top shut, while Jane stared at him in the most odd way. He felt the penguin soft and warm against his hand. Then he found the sandwiches. By good luck he pulled out a cucumber sandwich first time. Jane looked at it in disgust.

"It's been pecked!" she cried. "What have you got in there — an ostrich?"

"Don't be stupid, Jane," said Mum. "Just get on and eat it."

The penguin seemed rather upset by Jane's voice, because it began to squeak. Not very loudly, but loud enough to be heard by everybody. Dad was slowing down behind a lorry.

"Brakes have started squeaking," he growled.

"You'll have to oil them, Dad," suggested Jane. Tom pulled a face.

"You can't oil brakes, stupid. Then they wouldn't work at all." Dad laughed and said Tom was right. The penguin was quiet after that.

When they got home Tom said he was worn out. Mum suggested an early bed, so Tom crept upstairs, taking the duffle-bag with him. Mum wondered why he wanted all those old sandwiches but she was too tired to say anything and she soon forgot about it. In fact she dozed off and didn't wake until Dad brought her a cup of tea at half past nine.

"Why don't you have a bath and go to bed?" he said. "You look worn out."

Mum nodded and drank her tea. She went upstairs to run a bath. As she passed Tom's room she was surprised to hear him talking.

"That's right," he was saying. "You settle yourself down and we'll soon have you looking better. A nice bit of salmon sandwich — I expect you'll like that. Shall I tell you a story? How about *Jack and the Beanstalk*? Once upon a time there was a poor boy called . . . "

Mum pushed open the door and looked in. Tom was sitting up in bed. At the other end of the bed, also sitting up, was a penguin, carefully preening its feathers. "Tom! Dad!" screamed Mum. Dad came pounding up.

"Tom! What are you doing? Where did that penguin come from?"

"*Sssh!*" hissed Tom. "I was just going to tell it a story."

But Mum and Dad did not want to hear about Jack and the beanstalk. They wanted to know about the penguin, and Tom had to to tell them. As soon as he'd finished, Dad went to the telephone and rang the zoo. They were rather surprised to hear Dad's news and they promised to come and pick up the penguin in the morning. Dad explained to Tom how wrong it was to take penguins, even if Tom thought he was doing a good deed. Tom sighed and went to sleep, and the penguin spent that night in the bath with a tin of sardines that Mum had found in the kitchen.

Mum and Dad went to bed. "What are we going to do?" asked Dad. "Tom's determined to get an animal into this house." Mum lay thinking for a moment. Then she smiled.

"I wouldn't worry. I expect he'll forget all about it soon. Then it will be something else. What he really needs is a friend of his own age. Even a penguin is not much good for playing football with." Dad tried to smile. "I only hope you're right," he said.

Written by Jeremy Strong
illustrated by Bucket

47

Crazy Charlie

In the jungle, by the river, lived the biggest crocodile in the whole world. Crazy Charlie. That is what the other animals called him. He had the most enormous teeth and he ate everything he saw.

He started off in a small way, just munching the odd floating log or canoe. But then he got more ambitious and started to eat jetties and motor boats and bicycles.

In fact anything or anyone anywhere near the river at any time was in danger of being crunched up by Charlie's mighty teeth.

People all over the world were shocked and horrified, but this only made Crazy Charlie worse, because the more famous he became the more he showed off.

He started eating houses and trains and factories. Things had gone too far!

The people called in the Army. The soldiers showered Charlie with arrows, to frighten him away, but he caught them and used them as toothpicks.

They shot at him with cannon but Charlie caught the cannonballs and crunched them up like gobstoppers.

They even fired a guided missile at him, but he ate that too — and enjoyed it. The people were in despair. But Crazy Charlie was having the time of his life being the centre of the world's attention.

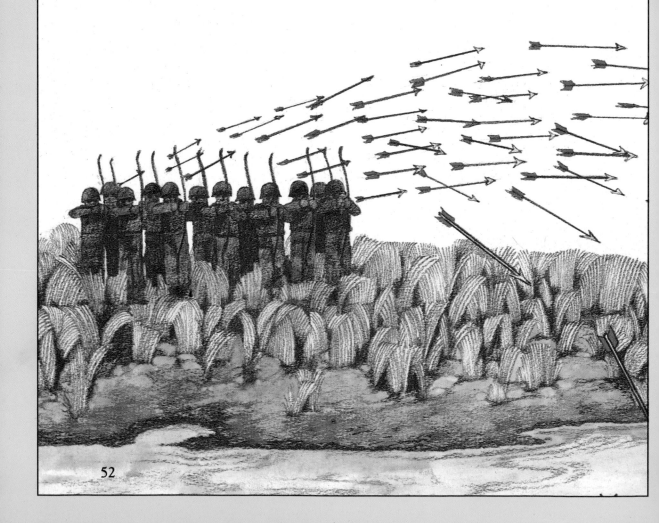

But one day something terrible happened to Charlie. One by one his huge, beautiful, sharp teeth began to fall out.

Finally he was totally toothless. The crowds didn't come any more; nobody was frightened of him; nobody made a fuss. He was no longer big news. Life was very dull for Crazy Charlie. But the other animals enjoyed the peace and quiet.

One day Charlie saw a tourist, the first he'd seen for about six months. The man, who was collecting plants, looked absolutely terrified when he stumbled over the crocodile dozing by the river.

But Charlie knew that there was no point in trying to frighten the man. Who's afraid of a gummy crocodile anyway? So he just gave him a toothless grin instead.

The man was so relieved that he smiled at Charlie. "I know just what you need," he said. "I'll send you some when I get home."

Charlie thought no more about him until a few months later when a large parcel arrived for him. It was from the plant-collecting tourist. He was a dentist and he had made Charlie the most beautiful set of sparkling teeth!

Charlie Crocodile.
The Jungle.

Crazy Charlie put them in his mouth and smiled the
shiniest smile anyone had ever seen. People started
flocking to see him once more, and how Charlie
loved it! He was big news again, the centre of the
world's attention, but now all he had to do was
SMILE.

Written and illustrated by Ruth Brown

SOME ANIMAL JOKES!

Q What's a crocodile's favourite game?

A Snap!

Q What's black, white and red?

A A sunburned penguin!

Q What dog can't bark?

A A hot dog!

Q Why don't elephants like penguins?

A Because they can't get the paper off!

Q Why did the horse stop tap dancing?

A Because it fell into the sink!

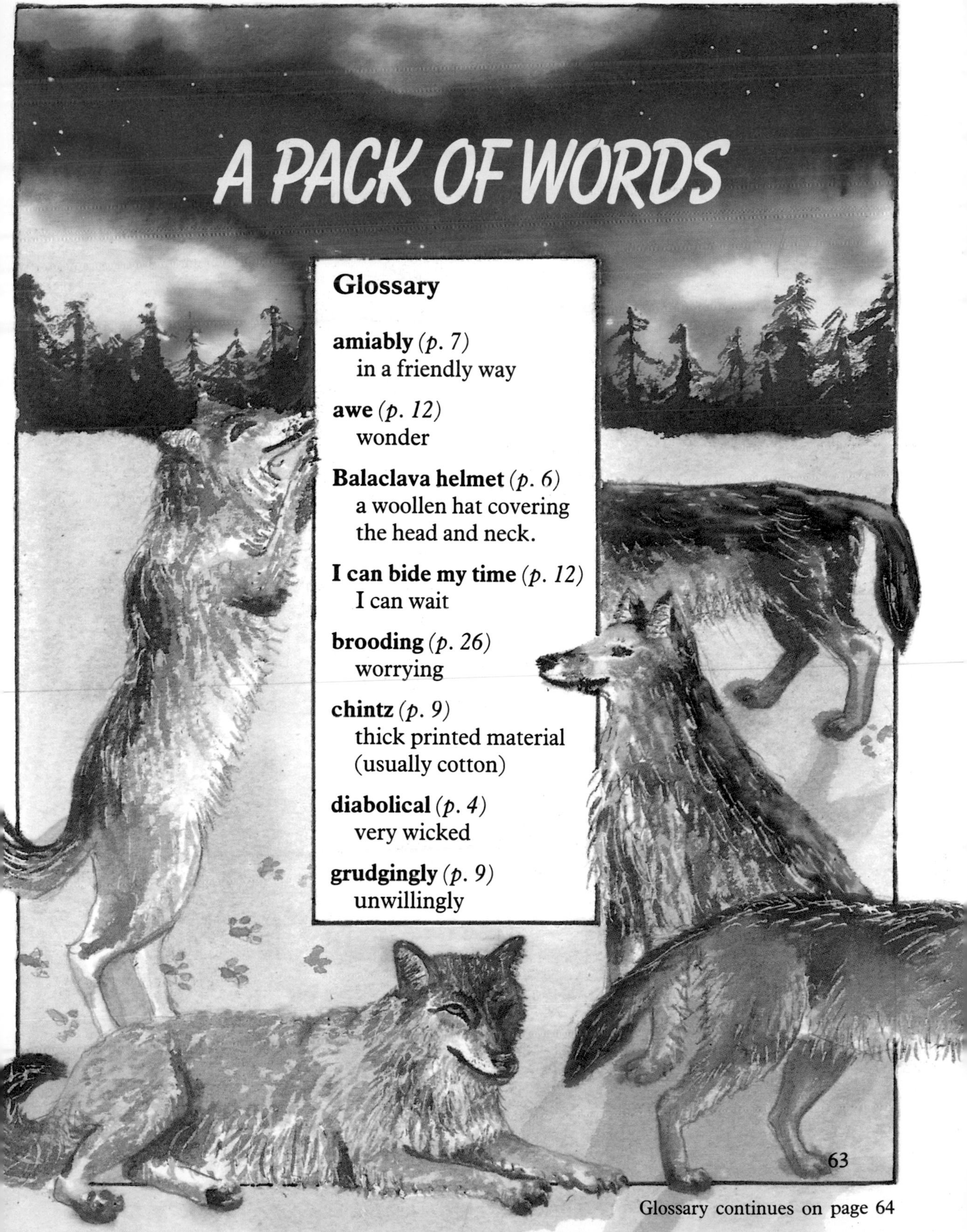

A PACK OF WORDS

Glossary

amiably *(p. 7)*
  in a friendly way

awe *(p. 12)*
  wonder

Balaclava helmet *(p. 6)*
  a woollen hat covering
  the head and neck.

I can bide my time *(p. 12)*
  I can wait

brooding *(p. 26)*
  worrying

chintz *(p. 9)*
  thick printed material
  (usually cotton)

diabolical *(p. 4)*
  very wicked

grudgingly *(p. 9)*
  unwillingly

63

Glossary continues on page 64

hesitated *(p. 21)*
stopped, paused

incurred four faults *(p. 11)*
made a mistake and
got four points against him

jetties *(p. 51)*
walkways built out
into the water,
used for getting
on and off boats

lurking *(p. 5)*
waiting in hiding,
for some bad purpose

preening its feathers *(p. 46)*
arranging its feathers
using its beak

ventriloquist *(p. 33)*
someone who can make
his or her voice
appear to come from
someone else

vibrated *(p. 4)*
shook